50 NIFTY SCIENCE EXPERIMENTS

Written by

Lisa Melton and Eric Ladizinsky

Illustrated by Neal Yamamoto

Copyright © 1990, 1992 by RGA Publishing Group, Inc.

All rights reserved. No part of this work may be reproduced or transmitted in any form or by any means, electronic or mechanical, including photocopying and recording, or by any information storage or retrieval system, except as may be expressly permitted by the 1976 Copyright Act or in writing by the publisher.

Manufactured in the United States of America.

ISBN: 1-56565-137-5
Library of Congress Cataloging-in-Publication Card No.: 92-6806

10 9 8 7 6 5 4 3 2

Lowell House
Juvenile
Los Angeles

Let's Get into the Swing of Things

PARENTAL SUPERVISION RECOMMENDED

You may have heard that energy cannot be lost or gained. The swing of a pendulum demonstrates this well. In the next experiment, you can prove to yourself that energy cannot be gained.

What You'll Need

- an empty shampoo or other plastic bottle, with screw-on cap
- string
- a ceiling hook
- water
- a partner

Directions

1. Find a hook attached to a ceiling or ceiling beam. The area around the hook should be cleared of any objects.
2. Take a piece of string that's long enough to tie around the hook and still reach your chest. Ask an adult to tie the string in place.
3. To make your pendulum, first fill the shampoo bottle with water to give it weight. Have a partner hold the bottle while you tie the hanging end of the string around its neck.
4. Now we'll test conservation of energy . . . and your nerve! Hold the bottle and back up with it until you can hold it as high as your nose (but don't touch it to your nose).
5. Now let go and stand very still. What happens? Did you flinch?

Why?

When you lifted the pendulum to your nose, you had to do a little work. When you then let go, all the effort you used to lift it went right into the pendulum. In other words, the pendulum swung with the same amount of energy as it took to lift it up. On its return swing, the pendulum could only come as high as you had lifted it before, because that's when it ran out of energy.

The amount of energy you give up is the amount of energy you get back. If, for example, someone had no money and you gave them a dollar, he or she could only give you a dollar back—that's conservation of energy.

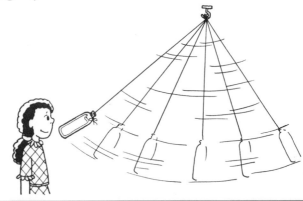

NOTE: The magnifying glass in the upper right-hand corner indicates the level of difficulty of each science experiment, from easy to hard.

A Swing in Time

Think back to the last time you played on a swing. Do you remember rising higher with each push from a friend? If your friend pushed at the *wrong* time, you wouldn't get anywhere. Knowing why holds the key to many things.

What You'll Need

- seven pieces of string (one 24″ long, two 12″ long, two 8″ long, and two 5″ long)
- two chairs of same height
- ruler
- six large nails

Directions

1. Tie either end of the longest string to the backs of the two chairs as shown. Pull the chairs apart so the string is tight.
2. Using the ruler to measure, tie the remaining strings approximately 3″ apart on the suspended string, in the order shown.
3. Next tie a nail to the end of each string. You now have six pendulums.
4. Lift one nail (any one you like) toward you, then let go and let it swing. Push the nail at just the right moment so it swings even higher. What happens? Another nail will start to swing. Which one?
5. Try swinging a different nail. Which other nail starts to swing this time?

Why?

Every pendulum has a natural, or resonant, frequency at which it swings when pushed. (Frequency refers to how many times the pendulum goes back and forth per second. The longer pendulums have a slower frequency than the shorter ones). When a pendulum is pushed at its natural frequency, it will rise higher and higher—just as a swing will when pushed at the right moment.

In your experiment, when you swung one pendulum (say, the 8″ one), small vibrations of the same frequency traveled across the suspended string. When they reached the other 8″ pendulum, they pushed it at the pendulum's natural frequency, so it started swinging, too.

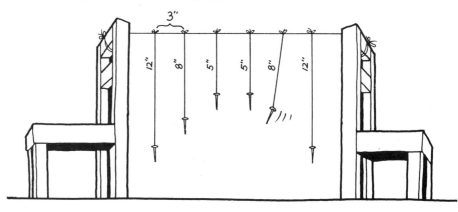

3

Become a Film Star

MEDIUM

EASY

HARD

In this experiment you'll amaze your friends with your film talents.

What You'll Need

- medium-sized bowl
- finely ground pepper
- a gullible friend
- water
- a bar of soap

Directions

1. Before the experiment, secretly wet your index finger and rub it along a bar of soap.
2. Fill a bowl about three-quarters full of water.
3. Shake the pepper over the water for a few seconds. The pepper will form a film over the water.
4. Say that you heard some humans have an energy field around them that repels pepper—but only certain *special* humans. Have your friend stick a finger into the water. Nothing will happen.
5. Now stick your soaped-up index finger into the water. Wow! *Your* energy field works great!

Why?

Of course, it was the soap film on your finger that repelled the pepper. When you put your finger in the water, the soap quickly spread out in a thin (invisible) layer. As it expanded outward, it pushed away the pepper.

Yolking Around

Would you like to give a friend a raw egg to eat but make him or her think it's really hard-boiled? Do the following experiment and you'll learn how.

What You'll Need

- fresh egg
- hard-boiled egg, cooled
- a gullible friend

Directions

1. Have someone mix up the fresh and hard-boiled eggs so you don't know which is which.
2. Now take one egg and spin it. Take note of how fast it spins. Spin it again, then stop the spin by putting your index finger on the egg for a second. What happens to the egg when you take your finger off?
3. Spin the second egg. Does it spin faster or slower than the first egg? Spin the egg again, then tap it with your finger to stop it. What happens to this egg when you take your finger off? Why does one egg keep spinning? Can you now tell which is the egg you can hand over to your friend and be certain there'll be a mess for him or her to clean?

Why?

When you're driving down the road in a car and suddenly come to a stop, did you ever notice how your body keeps going forward after the car stops? (This is the main reason for seatbelts, of course.) When something is moving, it will continue to move until something stops it. If two things are rigidly connected to each other, stopping one will stop the other.

In a fresh egg, you can think of the shell as the car and the yolk as your body. When the spinning egg comes to a halt, the yolk is free to keep spinning because it is not rigidly connected to the shell. With the hard-boiled egg, however, you can think of the entire egg as the car, because it's solid through and through. When you tap your finger on the egg to stop it, the yolk stops when the shell stops—it has a seatbelt on!

Gravity as a Pump

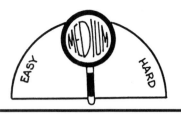

Have you ever thought about what you would do in a flood? How could you pump the water out of your house without a pump? We'll show you how to use the earth's gravitational pull to do exactly that.

What You'll Need

- approximately ten feet of transparent rubber tubing, ½" to ¾" in diameter
- kitchen sink
- large-sized pail
- food coloring (any color)
- ladder (or stack of books)
- chair

Directions

1. Coil the rubber hose and put it in your kitchen sink.
2. Plug up the drain, then start filling the sink with water. Add some food coloring so you can better watch the flow of water later.
3. As you fill the sink, hold up one end of the hose to the faucet to get all the air bubbles out of the hose as you fully immerse it.
4. Plug up both ends of the rubber hose with your thumbs and bring one of the ends into a pail on the floor (A). Make sure the end in the sink remains submerged.
5. When you've got your pump in place in the pail, take your thumbs off and watch what happens. Why does the water drain out of the sink?
6. Let the water drain completely into the pail (but not out of the hose). Now perform the experiment again, this time draining the water from the pail back into the sink. To demonstrate that gravity is at work, this time place the pail on a chair next to your sink. Will the water drain?
7. Now lift the pail higher by means of a ladder (or a stack of books placed on the counter under the pail). How high does the pail need to be before the water in it will drain into the sink?

Ⓐ

Just as your body wants to come back down after you jump up, the water in the sink wants to come down (since it is above ground level). But it can't, since the sink contains it. With the hose to drain it, the water now has a way of getting down. The bubbles in the hose push back against the water, preventing it from flowing freely. That's why you have to get all the bubbles out.

The distance from the sink to the pail needs to be greater than the distance from the sink to the top of the hose (B). If not, the water will not flow. Can you guess why? (The energy needed to pull the water up to the top of the hose would be greater than the amount of gravitational energy available.)

Also, the higher the pail of water, the faster the flow. As you lift the pail higher and higher, you give it more and more energy. The water also has a greater distance to fall and thus more time to gain speed. If you put the pail on top of a ladder outside and let the water drain to the ground, you'll see how quickly the pail is emptied of its water.

Wonder List

- You may think that gravity is a strong force, but compared to other forces (such as magnetic), it is very weak indeed. Consider this: when you jump into the air, for a split second you actually overcome the gravitational pull of the huge planet you're standing on!

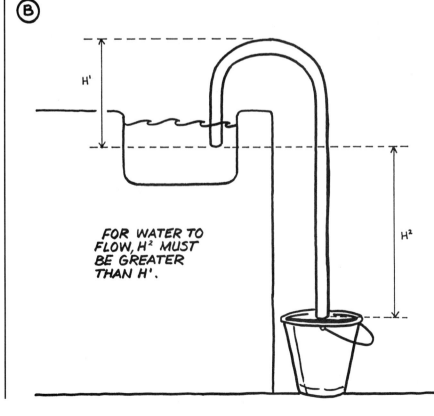

(B)

H¹

H^1

FOR WATER TO FLOW, H^2 MUST BE GREATER THAN H^1.

H^2

The Skater's Finale

PARENTAL SUPERVISION RECOMMENDED
As a last dazzling move, a figure skater will sometimes whirl in a tornadolike finish, spinning around faster than it seems possible—even on ice. How do skaters do it? Athletic skill has much to do with it, of course, but without a certain principle of science, the move couldn't be done. We'll let you observe this "hyper-spin" at work, then have you perform "the skater's finale."

What You'll Need

- two thread spools (without thread, or cover the thread with masking tape)
- approximately 30 inches of string (rawhide or a shoelace will do)
- pair of socks

Directions

1. Tie a knot in one end of the string, then pull it through the first spool so it rests on top of the knotted end.
2. Now pull the string through the second spool, leaving about four inches of string free at the unknotted end (A).
3. Find an open area to perform the experiment. Holding spool 2 with your left hand and the free end of the string with your right hand, swing spool 1 around as shown. When you've got it spinning fairly rapidly, note how fast it is spinning around.
4. Now stop spinning spool 1 and gently pull the string with your right hand (B). What happens to it? Can you explain why the spool spins faster?

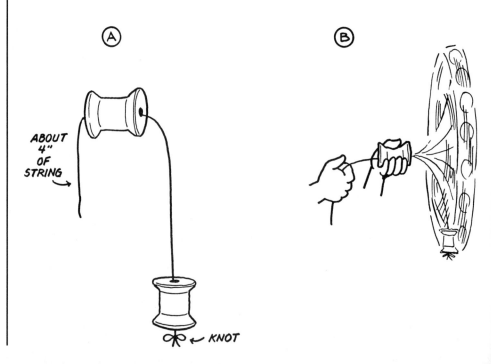

Ⓐ

ABOUT 4" OF STRING →

KNOT

Ⓑ

5. Now you're ready for your performance on "ice." Stand on a linoleum or wooden floor with your socks on and your arms spread out. Spin around on one foot like a skater doing a pirouette.
6. Keep your arms outstretched for a moment, then bring your arms in close to your body as you spin. Did you notice that you spun faster when you brought your arms in?
7. Now repeat the performance, this time holding a heavy book in each out-stretched hand before you start spinning. When you bring your arms in close this time, you'll notice that the whipping sensation is more intense.

Why?

In the first part of your experiment, why did spool 1 speed up? Well, since the spool was moving, it had a certain amount of energy. Then, when you pulled the string through spool 2, you did some work. This took energy, which you gave to spool 1. (Just as lifting the pendulum "handed over" energy to the pendulum, here, too, pulling the string handed over energy to the spool.) With more energy, the spool could speed up (C).

This same explanation can be used for your skating finale. Since you were spinning on the linoleum floor, you already had energy. Pulling your arms in took a little work. The energy from that work was transferred directly to your spin. So, you spun even faster. When you held the books in your hands, the effect became even more dramatic.

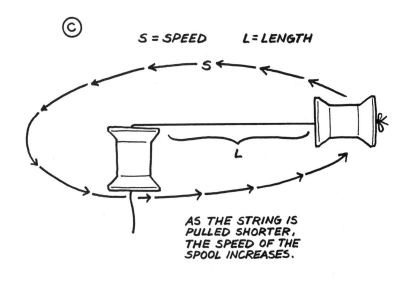

ⓒ

S = SPEED   L = LENGTH

AS THE STRING IS PULLED SHORTER, THE SPEED OF THE SPOOL INCREASES.

Instant Hercules I

You've heard of the ancient Roman hero and strongman, Hercules? After you've performed this experiment, you can join his ranks.

What You'll Need

- a fairly large, fresh potato
- paper straw

Directions

1. Holding the potato in one hand and the straw in the other, try to ram the straw through the potato. Tough to do, right?
2. Repeat the procedure, this time holding your thumb over one end of the straw and ramming with the other end. Wow! How did you get to be so strong?

Why?

When the end of the straw was uncovered and you rammed it into the potato, it was very easy for the straw's flimsy sides to collapse. But when you covered the straw with your thumb, you trapped air inside the straw, and that changed everything. As the straw entered the potato, the trapped air became compressed and pushed outward (like the way a compressed spring pushes outward) against the sides of the straw. The air prevented the straw from collapsing, and you could push it through the potato.

Instant Hercules II

PARENTAL SUPERVISION RECOMMENDED

When you understand a few simple ideas, you can perform physical feats that would otherwise be impossible. For example, using a lever, you can move a boulder much too heavy to lift by yourself. This experiment involves the lever—a machine that demonstrates the principle of "mechanical advantage."

What You'll Need

- medium-sized pail
- two 2″ nails
- water
- broom with long handle
- tall chair or bench
- hammer
- ruler

Directions

1. Fill the pail with water and find a spot outside. With one hand, try lifting the pail as high as your shoulder. Can you do it?
2. Now we'll use some mechanical advantage. Hammer the nails into the broom handle (not all the way), one about three inches from the end, the other about four inches. Then place the broom over the back of a chair and place the pail handle between the nails as shown.
3. Push on the opposite end of the broom and lift the pail. Was it easier to lift using the lever? How high can you lift the water?

Why?

Lifting the pail of water off the ground takes the same amount of energy no matter how the job is done, whether by hand or by lever. In your experiment, it was easier for you to lift the pail with the lever because it gave you mechanical advantage. However, using the lever did not mean that you *did less work*. It just meant that you used the same amount of energy in a different, easier way—namely, it took you *longer* to complete the job. Using a lever is a lot like taking a long, easy trail to the top of a hill rather than taking a short, steep trail. The shorter way seems like it takes more energy (because it's steep), but it doesn't. Even though each step on the easy trail takes little effort, there are many more steps to take. Whichever way you choose to get to the top (or lift the pail), the total amount of energy used is the same.

Give Me a Lift

PARENTAL SUPERVISION RECOMMENDED

If an airplane can weigh as much as 500,000 pounds, how does it manage to stay in flight? The reason has much to do with the principle of lift. In the next experiment, we'll demonstrate how airflow can create lift.

What You'll Need

- an 8″ x 11″ piece of heavy construction paper
- scissors
- protractor (or jar 4″ to 5″ in diameter)
- tape
- plastic straw
- ruler
- hole puncher (optional)

Directions

1. Using the protractor (or jar), construction paper, and scissors, cut out a circle with a 4″ or 5″ diameter.
2. Cut out another piece of paper, this time a square with 5″ sides. Set the square aside.
3. In the center of the circle, punch out a hole that's big enough for the straw to fit through. (If you don't have a hole puncher, use a pair of scissors to poke a hole through the paper, then twist the scissors around to increase the size of the hole.)
4. Put one end of the straw in the hole and carefully tape it in place as shown. (A). This is your blower.
5. Place the square piece of construction paper on a table and hold your blower about two inches above it. Now blow through the straw. As you might have expected, the paper was blown out of place.
6. Repeat the procedure, this time holding your blower about a half inch away. Blow hard on the straw and watch what happens. The square not only didn't get blown out of place, it got sucked up!

Ⓐ

TAPE STRAW
TO CIRCLE

Why? There is a principle in physics that describes how pressure relates to the flow of fluids (air is considered a fluid). The principle says that as a fluid in a stream moves faster, the pressure on its sides decreases. You can test this for yourself by turning on your garden hose and pinching in the sides. If the water is streaming out very fast, it will be easy to pinch in the sides of the hose. But if the water is streaming out slowly, it will be much harder to pinch the hose closed.

The same is true of air. You created a stream of moving air when you blew through the straw. When you held the square piece of paper two inches away from your blower, the air couldn't be directed into streams (A). However, when you held your blower much closer to the square, the air was pushed outward between the blower disk and the square, forming two streams of rapidly moving air (B). The fast-moving (low-pressure) airstreams between your blower and the square paper pushed down less than the slow (high-pressure) air beneath the square pushed up (believe it or not, there is a layer of air beneath the square). So, the high-pressure air from below pushed the square up—lift!

Wonder List

• Why do lightweight objects get sucked out of a car window at high speed?

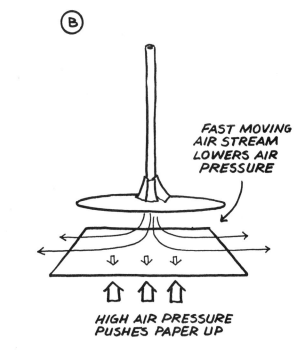

(B)

FAST MOVING
AIR STREAM
LOWERS AIR
PRESSURE

HIGH AIR PRESSURE
PUSHES PAPER UP

Winging It

In this experiment, we'll build a wing and see how its curvature creates the kind of airflow necessary for flight.

What You'll Need

- pencil
- ruler
- strip of paper, as wide as the ruler and 4″ long
- tape

Directions

1. Tape one edge of the strip to the ruler so that it lines up with the 1½″ mark. Tape the other edge down at the ruler's 5″ mark. The paper "wing" should have a bulge in it.
2. Balance the ruler across the pencil. Then push the ruler a little past the balance point, so the paper-wing end seesaws down and touches the table.
3. Now, lay your chin down at the opposite end of the ruler and blow toward the wing. The paper-wing end of the ruler lifts up. How did that happen?

Why?

The curve makes the top of the wing longer than the bottom of the wing. Therefore, the air on top has to flow faster than the air on the bottom (under the ruler) to arrive at the back of the wing at the same time. The fast air flowing over the top pushes down less than the air below pushes up—so up it goes!

The Un-Waterfall

EASY MEDIUM HARD

If held upside down, water in a pail will naturally pour out. Not always, though. Sometimes it's possible to defy gravity.

What You'll Need

- pail (or small bucket)
- water

Directions

1. Fill the pail about half full with water.
2. Now find an open area outside where you can perform the experiment. Start by swinging the pail at your side to build up momentum.
3. Then swing the pail around in circles, fast, like a baseball pitcher "winding up." Though swung upside down, the water won't spill out.

Why?

When you swung the pail up, the water started moving upward. Before it could reach its highest point, however, the pail got in the way, so you felt the water crashing upward into the bottom of the pail. This crashing accounts for the upward pull you felt on your arm. On the way down, the pail was moving faster downward than the water could naturally fall. So, the pail actually pushed the water from behind, and the water appeared to be stuck to the pail. Because the pail was always in front of (catching) the water moving upward, then pushing the water from behind, it seemed as if some mysterious force was holding the water in the pail.

Wonder List

- How can people successfully live in the zero gravity of outer space? One way is to simulate gravity. In the movie *2001: A Space Odyssey*, there was a giant spinning space station that looked like a wheel. Just as the water stayed pressed against the bottom of the pail, so, too, did the astronauts stay pressed against the floor of the space station—as if there was gravity.

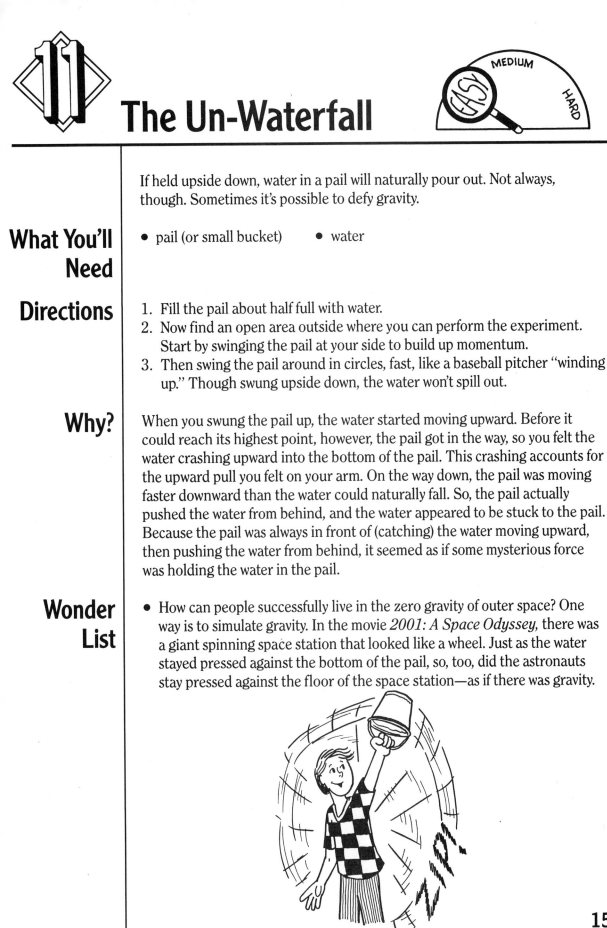

Tire in a Gyre

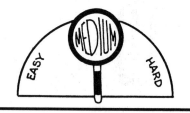

PARENTAL SUPERVISION RECOMMENDED
Have you ever wondered how your bike stays up when you ride it? Why don't you just fall over? Believe it or not, your bike has something in common with our planet.

What You'll Need

- bicycle tire
- ceiling hook
- a partner
- string

Directions

1. Have a parent help you remove a wheel from your bicycle.
2. Hold the bolts on either side of the center of the tire (the axis) and have someone spin it as hard as they can (A). You've just made a gyroscope.
3. Now try to move your hands up, down, right, and left while holding the gyroscope. What happens? Feels pretty weird, doesn't it!
4. Next, attach the wheel at one bolt to the same string and ceiling hook you used in the Swing of Things pendulum experiment.
5. Hold the wheel parallel to the ground and spin it hard. Holding the two bolts, lift it (with arm movement this time, not hand movement) to a different angle and let go (B). What happens? The gyroscope will maintain its position no matter how you angle it, even vertically.

Why?

The strange forces you felt in trying to move the spinning wheel have to do with an interesting property of gyroscopes. When you push on something, it usually moves in the direction you pushed it. For instance, if you grab the ends of the bike-wheel axis and push forward (while it is not turning), the wheel will move forward. However, when you push on the axis of a *spinning* wheel (a gyroscope), it does not move in the direction you push it. Instead, it moves to the side. That's because the spinning redirects the force pushed against the wheel.

13 You Can't Blow It

EASY / MEDIUM / HARD

It's easy enough to blow up a balloon. But what if the balloon is submerged under water? If deep enough, you'll find you just can't blow it.

What You'll Need

- two plastic straws
- bathtub filled with water
- a twist tie (like the ones used on plastic bags)
- balloon
- masking tape

Directions

1. Fit one end of a plastic straw into another to double the length of the straw. Seal the joint with masking tape.
2. Now insert one end of your double-straw into a deflated balloon. Push it all the way in until it is *almost* touching the opposite end of the balloon.
3. Wrap the twist tie around the lip of the balloon and tighten it (so that no air can escape the balloon when you blow it up).
4. Hold the double-straw and blow up your balloon. Notice how hard you had to blow to inflate it. It should be fairly easy.
5. Put the balloon under water as shown and try to blow it up again. Was it easier or harder to blow up the balloon while it was submerged?

Why?

You may not notice it, but there is air pressure pushing against you at all times. That pressure is the weight of the entire earth's atmosphere pressing down on you. Although our atmosphere is a whopping 300 miles high, it doesn't crush you because air is so light. Water, however, is much heavier than air—so much heavier, in fact, that only 33 feet of it is as heavy as 300 miles of air. This explains the problem in blowing up the submerged balloon. To blow up a balloon in air, the sides of the balloon must push out against the air pressure pushing in. This is easy for your lungs to do. But under water, the pressure increases dramatically. It's very difficult to push the sides of the balloon out against the water pressure pushing in.

Wonder List

- When diving, why do you need scuba equipment? Why not just use a long snorkel?

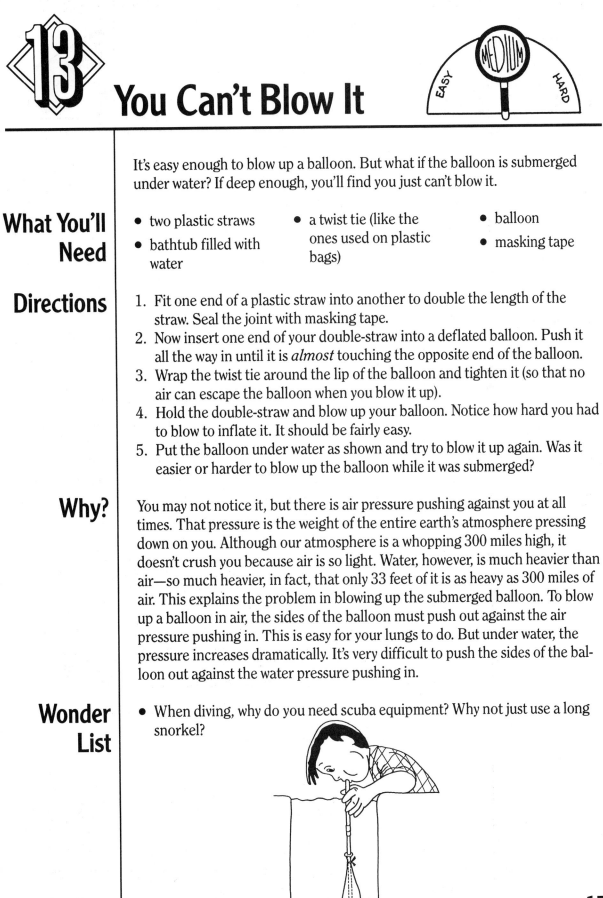

14 Boiling at Low Pressure

PARENTAL SUPERVISION REQUIRED

We usually think that a liquid boils because it's very hot. Usually, that's true. But not always . . .

What You'll Need

- 500-ml Erlenmeyer flask from a chemist's shop or toy store (with rubber stopper)
- 4 gallons of water chilled overnight in the refrigerator
- stove burner
- potholder glove
- kitchen sink with stopper
- tap water

Directions

1. Fill the Erlenmeyer flask to the 200-ml mark with tap water.
2. Pour the chilled water into your stopped-up kitchen sink.
3. Now set the flask on a stove burner. When the water is boiling, hold the flask with the potholder glove and carry it over to the sink. Place the stopper in the flask and tap it once. (Don't push the stopper in!)
4. Now, holding the flask by the stopper, put it all the way into the chilled water so it sits on the bottom of the sink. Keep your fingers on the stopper to hold the flask down. What happens to the water? It keeps on boiling!
5. *After five minutes,* take the stopper out and pour the boiling water out into your hand. It's only warm water!

Why?

The water will boil as long as the stopper remains in place. Why? Boiling occurs when the temperature of a liquid is high enough for bubbles to be able to push out against the weight of the air pushing down. The higher the temperature of the liquid, the more forcefully the bubbles can push out.

When your flask was covered and cooled by the chilled water, the air pressure in the flask dropped lower and lower. As a result, the air pushed less and less on the water below, making it easy for the bubbles in the water to push out (or boil). In other words, the lower the air pressure, the lower the boiling temperature, even if the water is ice cold.

Air Apparent I

PARENTAL SUPERVISION RECOMMENDED

If you can't see the air, how do you know it's there? We take the air's existence for granted, but the ancient Greeks didn't. They wanted to *prove* its existence. Through an experiment very similar to the one you're about to perform (without the plastic soft-drink bottle!), the Greeks did just that. They proved not only that air existed, but that it also exerted pressure.

What You'll Need

- a two-liter, plastic soft-drink bottle with metal cap
- hammer
- nail
- water

Directions

1. With the hammer and nail, punch one hole in the metal cap and one in the side of the bottle, about five inches from the bottom.
2. Now fill the bottle halfway and screw on the cap. Holding the bottle with both hands, turn it upside down. What happens? The water pours out in a steady stream (A).
3. Next, with the bottle still held upside down, cover the hole in the side of the container with your thumb (B). (Be sure not to squeeze the bottle.) What happens now?

Why?

When you turned the bottle upside down and allowed water to pour out, air came in through the punched hole in the side to replace the lost liquid. The air rushing in pushed out more liquid. When you closed up the hole, no air was allowed into the bottle to replace the water. The stream of water quickly came to a stop because the air inside the bottle didn't push as strongly against the water as the air outside the bottle pushed against the cap to keep the water in.

16

Air Apparent II

By defying gravity, we'll show another way to prove air exerts pressure.

What You'll Need

- plastic cup (no larger than 16 ounces)
- plastic or Styrofoam dinner plate
- water

Directions

1. Set the cup in your sink and fill it with water until it's overflowing.
2. Place the plate face down on the cup.
3. Now, holding the cup in one hand (without squeezing it) and, lightly pressing the plate to the cup with your other hand, turn the cup and plate over.
4. Take your hand off the plate and watch what happens. Wow—nothing! Now gently squeeze the cup.

Why?

Though it may be hard to believe, the weight of the water in the cup does not push as hard *down* on the plate as the air pressure below the plate pushes it *up*. It's as simple as that.

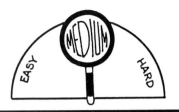

The Air Also Rises

PARENTAL SUPERVISION REQUIRED
Have you ever seen a beautiful hot-air balloon sailing gracefully in the sky?
What keeps it up? It's all in the name.

What You'll Need

- two brown paper lunch bags
- candle
- matches
- ruler
- tape
- one 18″ string, two 12″ strings

Directions

1. Tie the longer string around the middle of the ruler (at 6″ mark) and tape it in place.
2. Tape the other two pieces of string to the bottom of both bags (at center). Then tie the free end of the strings (with bags attached) to the ruler, one at the 1″ mark, one at the 11″ mark. Tape the strings in place on the ruler.
3. Tape the free end of the long piece of string to the underside of a doorframe.
4. Now light the candle and hold it under one bag. What happens?

Why?

A bagful of hot air is lighter than the same amount of cool air. Thus, the bag filled with hot air rises.

Wonder List

- On a hot day, would the air be cooler near the floor or near the ceiling?

High-Wire Act

PARENTAL SUPERVISION RECOMMENDED

Why do you suppose the brave people who walk the high wire at the circus use a balancing bar? We'll let you perform your own act and see.

What You'll Need

- two identical forks
- cola or vinegar bottle
- needle
- cork (about ¾" thick at bottom)
- pencil with eraser
- quarter

Directions

1. Place the quarter on top of the bottle opening.
2. Stick the eye of the needle in the center of the bottom of the cork.
3. Now stick the two forks into either side of the cork as shown.
4. Place your high-wire act on the quarter, needle down (A). How long will it stay balanced? Spin it around and bob it up and down like a seesaw. Set the needle on a pencil eraser (no need to push it in) and tilt the pencil in different directions (B). You've got a great balancing act on your hands.

Why?

On a seesaw, the farther you are seated from the center, the harder you push up the other side as you push down. The same principle is at work in your high-wire act. When one fork was tilted down one way, the other fork was lifted up away from the bottle. The lifted fork then pulled down hard to lift the other fork back up. In this way, the needle is kept balanced.

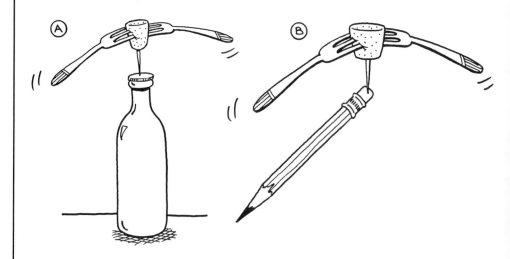

19 Oil & Water (& Air) Don't Mix

If oil and water (and let's not forget air) don't mix, do you suppose that light travels through them in the same way, or at the same speed?

What You'll Need

- tall, clear glass
- water
- pencil (as tall as the glass)
- cooking oil

Directions

1. Fill the glass three-quarters with water.
2. Pour about one-quarter cup oil into the water. The oil won't want to mix and will bead and float to the surface.
3. Now drop the pencil into the glass. What do you see? The pencil seems to have broken into three pieces.

Why?

Light travels faster in some materials than it does in others. As light travels from one material to another, if it changes speed, it can also change direction (or bend). In your experiment, one edge of the light wave hit the oil boundary first and slowed down. This caused the light wave to change direction. That same light wave then hit the water boundary. It again slowed and changed direction. Since the light is bent, your eye sees the pencil's image as bent.

OIL SETTLES ON TOP

WATER

Reflections on Color

Look around. The world about you (your room, the backyard, the playground) is filled with different colors. Did you know that all these different colors are made of various combinations of just three colors? Can you guess what these "primary" colors are? If you guessed red, yellow, and blue, you'd be right. Let's experiment with color.

What You'll Need

- heavy white drawing or construction paper
- measuring spoons
- medium-sized paintbrush (or use your fingers!)
- red, yellow, and blue tempera paints

Directions

1. Begin by pouring out globs of red, yellow, and blue paint (about a teaspoon each) on the construction paper.
2. Now mix your palette of colors. Start by mixing red with yellow. What color do you get? Wash your paintbrush out, then mix the red with the blue, and then the blue with the yellow. What colors do you get? (Save the colors you created for the Color Wheels experiment.)
3. Next, mix the red, yellow, and blue together. Looks pretty yucky, doesn't it? Experiment by adding various amounts of the three primary colors and you should get . . . black! Would you have guessed that red plus yellow plus blue equals black?

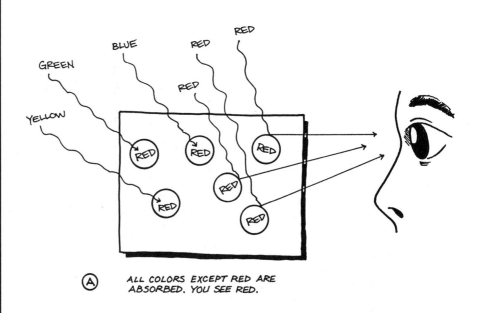

(A) ALL COLORS EXCEPT RED ARE ABSORBED. YOU SEE RED.

Why?

When you mix only two primary colors together, you get a "secondary" color. (The orange, green, and purple you mixed are secondary colors.) When you mix *three* primary colors together, why do you get black? The answer has to do with the way materials—all materials—reflect or absorb the colors of the light spectrum. For example, when you see a green leaf, it is absorbing all the spectral colors *except* green (A). In other words, the leaf is reflecting the color green.

Paint is no different than leaves when it comes to color. A glob of red paint absorbs all colors of the spectrum except red. Yellow paint absorbs all colors except yellow, and blue absorbs all but blue. When you mix these colors together, the net result is that *no color* is reflected—in other words, black (B).

Now that you know how to mix colors, your artist's canvas awaits you, Michelangelo!

Wonder List

- In what way is a black hole like a glob of black paint? Because of its incredibly strong gravitational pull, black holes "absorb" light and don't let any reflect back out.

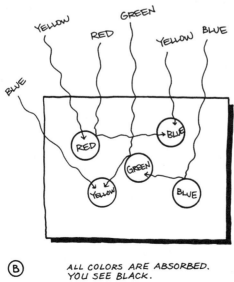

(B) ALL COLORS ARE ABSORBED.
YOU SEE BLACK.

Glass-Bottom Boat

Why do tropical cruise boats have glass bottoms? Why do scuba divers wear masks? Let's take a look.

What You'll Need

- large, clean plastic garbage can
- water
- clear glass pie dish or bowl
- various household items

Directions

1. Fill the garbage can with water.
2. Now you get to make your garbage can "party mix." Toss an apple, an orange, a comb, a tin box, a colorful coffee mug—anything that will sink but won't get waterlogged—into the can.
3. Look at your mix at the bottom of the garbage can. How well can you see all that stuff? If you're really daring, poke your head *into* the water and look again. It should be even harder to see the things at the bottom.
4. Now place the pie dish or bowl on top of the water and look again. Can you see any better?

Why?

The surface of a pool of water has bumps and movements that are difficult to see through. (When you put your face in the water, your vision was even worse because your eyes are designed to see not through water but through air.) Placing the glass bowl on the water flattens the water into a smooth surface. Light rays from a flat surface let your eyes focus much more easily.

Phantom Candles

PARENTAL SUPERVISION RECOMMENDED
Create a mysterious illusion in the next experiment, and discover how light interacts with a surface to make phantom images.

What You'll Need

- transparent plastic or acrylic plate (1 sq. ft. x ¼")
- matches
- two matching candle-holders, with two candles of equal size (not longer than 8")
- two narrow books of equal width

Directions

1. Start by placing the two books flat on a table, binder to binder, in a darkened room. Stand the plastic plate between the books.
2. Place one candle (in holder) on each book, about four inches away from the plastic. If there are handles in the holders, line them up so they're facing the same direction.
3. Now light the candles. Standing behind one candle, look through the plastic plate to the other candle. Make sure the candles are lined up.
4. Remove candle 2 from behind the plate, leaving its candleholder behind. A phantom candle appears in the empty candleholder!

Why?

You can see an object only by the light reflected by it. If no light can pass through it from behind, the object will appear solid. If light can pass through it *and* reflect off it, the object will appear ghostlike. In your experiment, the plastic allowed light reflected off of candleholder 2 to pass through it. It also reflected some of candle 1's light back to you, creating a ghostlike image of the candle in candleholder 2. Note: The reflection in the plastic will appear as far *behind* the plastic as the true object is in *front* of it.

Wonder List

- If you want to create a more dramatic phantom image, place two identical chairs on opposite sides of a glass door, at equal distances from it. Then, holding a candle in the dark, seat yourself in one of the chairs.

CANDLEHOLDER #1   CANDLEHOLDER #2

 **Why Isn't the Sky Green?**

We take for granted that the sky is blue, but why is it so? Why does it change color from dawn to noon to dusk? And why isn't it purple or green, or even colorless? As every good scientist knows, there are reasons for everything.

What You'll Need

- glass fishbowl (or a deep glass bowl)
- water
- flashlight
- two thick books
- measuring spoon
- milk

Directions

1. Fill the bowl with water and set it on a table in a darkened room.
2. Stir in two tablespoons of milk and you have recreated the sky.
3. Place the flashlight on the books about three feet away from the bowl. Shine the light directly into the "sky."
4. Crouch down and look into the bowl at eye level with the light behind you (but not blocked). What color does the "sky" appear?
5. Move slowly around the bowl until you're at the opposite side. Look through the bowl to the flashlight. What color is the "sky" now? It's amazing what a little more distance from the light will do!
6. Try holding the flashlight in your hand near the bowl now. What colors do you see as you move the light around and above the bowl?

Why?

Remember that light behaves like waves in many ways. We can understand why the sky is blue by looking at how ocean waves are affected by obstacles. Think about a wave of water moving on the surface of the water. If the wave hits a rock on the water, two different things can happen: If the rock is much smaller than the wave, the wave doesn't even notice and continues in the same direction almost completely unaffected. But if the rock is the same size or even larger than the wave, the wave bounces off and is thrown in a different direction. This effect is called "scattering."

Scattering is what happens to light in the earth's atmosphere. The air molecules are like the rocks, and the different colors of light are the different-sized waves. (Unlike ocean waves, however, unless light gets scattered, you can't see it.) Red light is made of big waves. Since the air molecules are small compared to these, the red light travels through the air without being scattered about. The same holds true for yellow and green light. Blue light, however, is made up of much smaller waves. When they hit the air molecules, they are bounced off in all directions. The result is that everywhere you look, you see blue.

At sunrise and sunset, when the sun is close to the horizon, the light reaching us travels through a greater thickness of atmosphere than when the sun is high overhead, where the air is thinner. When the atmosphere is thick, it contains more dust, air molecules, and water vapor with which to scatter light. The blue light (and green, too!) is scattered so much that we can't see it anymore. But now we are able to see the orange and red light, whose large waves can be scattered by the thick air.

Wonder List

- On Mars, the particles in the air are much bigger than in our atmosphere. So, the longer red waves crash into the air molecules and get scattered about. That's why the Martian sky appears red.

Getting Nowhere

PARENTAL SUPERVISION RECOMMENDED

Picture a spinning bicycle wheel. You can usually tell the direction in which it's spinning, but if the wheel is going fast enough, a strange thing happens. The wheel may actually appear to stop or, even more strangely, to spin backward.

What You'll Need

- heavy white cardboard or matte board (10″ x 10″ or larger)
- one long nail (about 2″ long and thin enough to fit inside spool)
- three small nails

- black felt pen
- piece of board (1 sq. ft. or larger), at least ½″ thick
- scissors
- spool of thread (2″ high)

- ruler
- protractor
- screw
- pencil
- any kind of tape
- string (18″ long)

Directions

1. Using the scissors, pencil, and protractor, cut a circle (5″ diameter) out of the cardboard. Mark the center of the circle.
2. With the ruler, draw four lines through the center of the "wheel" to create eight sections of equal size. Fill in four of the pie-shaped pieces with the black felt pen. Add a black dot to one empty pie piece (A).
3. Tape the thread on the spool in place so it won't unravel. Then poke the long nail all the way through the center of the top side of the wheel. Now drop the nail through the center of the spool (B).
4. Holding the paper and spool in place, nail the three small nails into the spool to secure it in place (C). Turn the wheel so the spool faces up, and the long nail will fall out.
5. Poke the nail through the circle about one-half inch from the outside of the wheel. Feed the string through this hole (C).

Ⓐ

Ⓑ

POKE NAIL THROUGH CENTER OF WHEEL AND DROP ONTO SPOOL

TAPE THREAD IN PLACE

6. Tie a "grip knot" on the wheel side of the string. On the spool side of the string, tie another knot, this one around a screw. (The screw acts as a weight.) Tape the screw in place on the underside of the wheel (C).
7. Drive the long nail through the board, and set the spool on top of it (C).
8. Hold the grip knot and gently turn the wheel around in circles. As you turn it faster and faster, what happens to the pie pieces on the wheel? Experiment with spinning the wheel at different speeds. At certain speeds, why do the pie pieces appear to go backward?

Why?

Your brain can perceive (or see) motion only so fast. If an object is moving faster than that, you will only see parts of it. Your brain can observe twenty-four changes in motion per second. Movies are a good example of this. For every second you watch a movie, twenty-four frames whiz by. If there were fewer or more than twenty-four frames, the action would seem unnatural.

As you sped up your spool-wheel, at one point it simply spun too fast for your brain to see. Before then, your brain could observe the full motion of the wheel. But why would the wheel appear to go backward? For one thing, the wheel would have to be going fast enough (say, several cycles per second) so you couldn't follow the black dot as it traveled around it. Then, let's say that the last split-second your brain saw the wheel was when the black dot was pointing toward noon. If the next time you saw the wheel the dot was not clockwise of noon, but, say, at 11 o'clock, the wheel would appear to be going backward. If the next time your brain sees the dot it's at 10 o'clock, then 9 o'clock, and so forth, the wheel will seem to be going backward.

Wonder List

- A strobe light has the reverse effect of the spinning spool-wheel. Instead of giving your brain too much information to perceive, the strobe light, in blacking out portions of information, gives your brain too little to perceive.

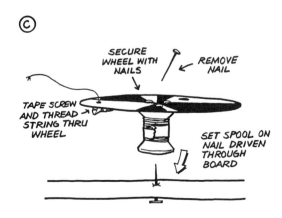

Ⓒ

SECURE WHEEL WITH NAILS

REMOVE NAIL

TAPE SCREW AND THREAD STRING THRU WHEEL

SET SPOOL ON NAIL DRIVEN THROUGH BOARD

Color Wheels

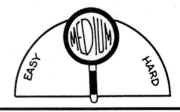

PARENTAL SUPERVISION RECOMMENDED
Now let's examine how your brain *sees* colors. We don't mean in just an ordinary way, but when you set your colors spinning.

What You'll Need

- paints (primary and secondary colors)
- paintbrush
- protractor (or dinner plate for tracing)
- transparent tape
- scissors
- pencil
- white construction paper
- the spool-wheel and board you made in the Getting Nowhere experiment

Directions

1. Using a pencil, scissors, and a protractor, cut out several circles of white construction paper.
2. Draw lines down the center of your "wheels," separating them into halves.
3. On one circle, paint one half red and the other half green.
4. When the wheel is dry, attach it onto the spool-wheel with the tape. Make sure to put tape on either side of the string, which should come out the side between the two wheels (A).
5. Grab the string and spin the wheel faster and faster. What happens to the green and red?
6. Repeat steps 3 through 5, this time painting a wheel blue and orange, then one yellow and purple. What happens to the colors?

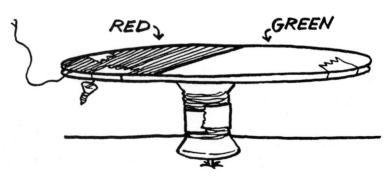

Ⓐ

RED   GREEN

Why?

As you learned in Getting Nowhere, when you look at something, your brain keeps a picture of it inside your head for a little while. This is called "persistence of vision." You can see this by grabbing one end of a pencil between two fingers and quickly wiggling it in front of you. If you shake the pencil fast enough, it will appear as if there are two pencils (B). Of course, you know there's only one—the "second" pencil is merely the persistent image inside your head of the real pencil. Your brain hasn't had time to get rid of the first picture before it sees the pencil moved to another position. This is why fast-moving objects appear to blur.

When you turned your color wheel fast enough, your brain didn't have time to get rid of one color before it saw the next color. So, your brain simply combined the two color pictures, just like it combined the two pencil pictures. The interesting thing is that your brain sees rapid, alternating pictures of red and green as white, blue and orange as white, and yellow and purple as gray!

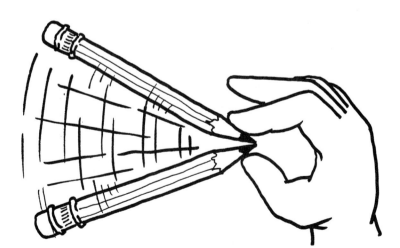

Light Dispersion

Centuries ago, Sir Isaac Newton made an incredible discovery: light wasn't white at all, but actually many colors of light that combined to look white. This was a major discovery in the field of optics (the study of light). We know a great deal about our universe through the study of the light spectrum.

What You'll Need

- prism
- sheet of white paper
- lamp (without shade)

Directions

1. Experiment with the prism in normal light by holding it up to your eye and viewing several objects. You'll see that the light reaching your eye from these objects *disperses,* or separates, into colors.
2. Now hold up a piece of paper near the lamp light, and look at its edges through the prism. How many different colors can you see?

Why?

In outer space (in a vacuum), all the different colors in a beam of light travel at the same speed. As a result, they stay combined and are seen as white light. But when light travels through glass, the different colors travel at *different* speeds. One color outruns another, and they begin to separate. As they spread out, they can be seen individually. It's just like running a race. If everyone runs at the same speed, they will stay together. If everyone runs at different speeds, pretty soon the runners are all spread out, just like the different colors of light in a prism.

Wonder List

- Almost everything we know about in outer space—how big stars are, what they're made of—comes from studying the various colors of light given off by stars. This area of study is called "spectrum analysis."
- You can see the spectrum—a rainbow—by spraying a fine mist from your garden hose into the air with the sun behind you.

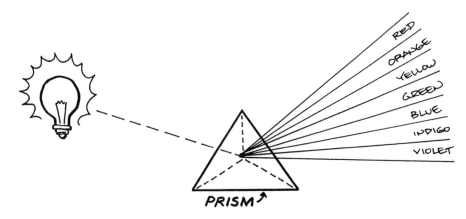

It's the Wave!

We know that white light can split into its various colors, but can it disappear into blackness? (And we don't mean by turning off the light switch!) Read on.

What You'll Need

- nylon stockings (black or another dark color works best)

Directions

1. Take one stocking leg and hold it up to the light as shown. Notice the patterns and waves of light and dark?
2. Stretch the nylon in different directions and see the patterns change.

Why?

Many things in nature behave like the waves in the ocean. When two waves smash into each other, they form a bigger wave. If a bump in a wave collides with a dip in the wave, the wave disappears. This "disappearing wave" is easy to understand if you compare it to a hole in the ground. The dirt dug out of the hole forms a mound (bump) next to the hole (dip). The mound is like the crest of the wave, and the hole is like the trough. When a mound meets a hole, the mound fills the hole, and what are you left with?

Light also travels in waves. Just as a bump and dip in the water can make each other disappear, so can two light waves. You can't see the light waves, but you can see how a material affects them. When the light traveled through the nylon mesh, it combined in all these ways: bump to bump, dip to dip, and bump to dip. These interactions are called interference. When a light bump fell into a light dip, the light disappeared—darkness. These are the dark areas you saw. The light areas are where two bumps or two dips combined.

Wonder List

- Two sound waves can cancel each other out and produce . . . silence.
- Interference patterns are used to create three-dimensional holographic images.

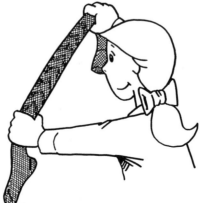

Optical Illusions

Optical illusions help reveal how your brain works. Sometimes your brain will interpret an unfamiliar image as being familiar, even though it's *mis*interpreting it. That's why optical illusions are fun—you get to catch your brain making a mistake! Look at these illusions and see if you can figure out why your brain mistakes what it sees.

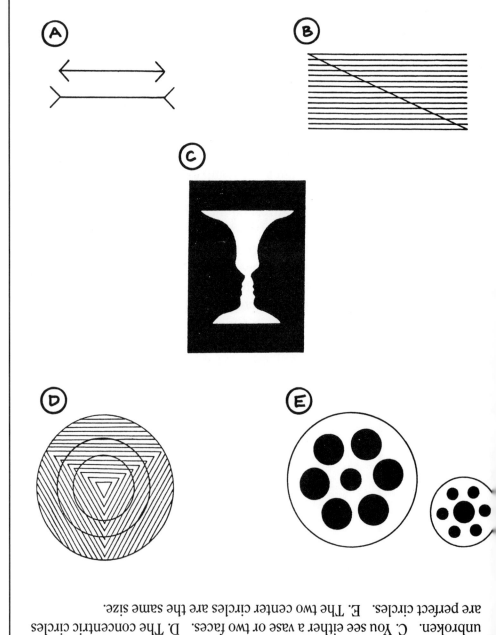

A. Both lines are the same length.   B. the diagonal line is straight and unbroken.   C. You see either a vase or two faces.   D. The concentric circles are perfect circles.   E. The two center circles are the same size.

What's the Sense of It?

You know the world around you only through your senses. But did you know that your senses can sometimes fool you, giving you a misleading picture of the world? In this experiment, we'll explore the sensation of touch.

What You'll Need

- three large bowls
- ice cubes
- a clock or watch with second hand
- water

Directions

1. Fill the bowls with water: the first bowl with very hot water (not boiling), the second with lukewarm water, the third with ice water.
2. Dunk your left hand into the hot water and your right hand into the ice water at the same time. Have a partner clock fifteen seconds while you keep your hands fully immersed.
3. Now place both hands into the lukewarm water at the same time. What happens? How would you describe the sensation your left hand feels? What about your right hand?

Why?

Sometimes your senses measure something very different than you think they do. For example, you may think that what feels hot has a high temperature or that what feels cold has a low temperature. But your body doesn't measure temperature. (If it did, when you placed your hands in the lukewarm water they would have felt the temperature as the same, but they didn't.) What you feel, instead, is the *change* in temperature and how fast that change is occurring—that is, how fast you receive or give away heat energy.

Receiving heat feels hot, and the faster you receive it, the hotter it feels. Giving heat away feels cool, and the faster you give it away, the cooler it feels. Since heat always travels from the hotter object to the cooler object, your cold right hand received heat from the lukewarm water, so it felt warm. Your warm left hand gave away heat to the lukewarm water, so it felt cool.

COLD   LUKEWARM   HOT

Sweet-and-Sour Science

Do you know where your sweet, salty, sour, and bitter taste centers are? Let's explore the sense of taste and answer this question.

What You'll Need

- sugar
- instant coffee grains
- vinegar
- measuring spoons
- cap from vinegar bottle
- table salt
- plate

Directions

1. Pour your ingredients into separate piles on a plate. You'll need a quarter teaspoon each of salt, sugar, and coffee, and a capful of vinegar.
2. Wet your finger, dip it into the salt and place your finger in the center of your tongue—not too far forward and not too far back. Keep your finger in place and your mouth open (closing your mouth will spread the taste to other parts of your tongue). Can you taste anything?
3. Now move your finger to a salty taste center. What happens now?
4. Repeat steps 2 and 3 with the sugar, coffee, and vinegar. (For best results, rinse your mouth out before moving on to a new taste.) When experimenting with sugar, move your finger to the tip of your tongue; with the coffee, to the back of your tongue; and with the vinegar, to either side and slightly back. Did you taste anything by touching the center of your tongue? What about when you moved your finger and struck a taste center?

Why?

Did you know that all tastes—from banana to barbecue chicken to cheddar cheese—are a combination of any or all of the four "primary" tastes (remember the Reflections on Color experiment)? You can test this by creating a combo-taste. Dip one finger into the sugar and the other into the vinegar. Now place both fingers in your mouth at the same time and close your mouth. Can you taste the sugar and vinegar mixing? Does it remind you of a Chinese dish you had recently? Presto—sweet-and-sour finger!

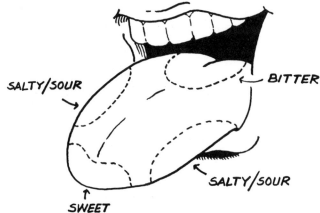

31 Tickle Your Feet

EASY MEDIUM HARD

Why can't you tickle yourself? If someone else tickles you, why do you become unbearably ticklish? The answers are not as easy as you think!

What You'll Need

• a ticklish partner

Directions

1. Working with a partner, try to tickle yourselves in your most ticklish spots. Not much fun, is it?
2. Now it's time to tickle each other for a minute or two. If you were paying attention, your partner identified his or her tickle "hot spot," so . . . one, two, three, go!
3. After the two of you have recovered, try to explain why you couldn't tickle yourself but your partner could. Any ideas?

Why?

One reason for not being able to tickle yourself is physical. When you tickle yourself, your brain has two streams of touch sensations to deal with: those coming from the area you're tickling, and those coming from the hand doing the tickling. When *someone else* tickles you, your brain has only one stream of sensations to process. Your brain can concentrate on the tickling sensations alone. But believe it or not, tickling has more to do with psychology than with your sensation of touch. When someone else is about to tickle you, there are a few silly seconds of anticipation before the tickling begins. This anticipation makes your brain focus attention on the tickling sensations you're about to experience. You "tune in" more, so you actually have a heightened experience of the sensations.

Invisible Ink

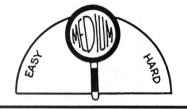

PARENTAL SUPERVISION REQUIRED

Treasure maps and scientific formulas, escape plans and code secrets—you can't let just anybody see these things. No, for these kinds of schemes, you just have to have invisible ink!

What You'll Need

- bottled lemon juice
- paintbrush
- very long stick matches
- notebook paper

Directions

1. Make up a secret message for your best friend. Then, with the paintbrush and lemon juice, paint your message on the paper.
2. Set the paper aside to dry (sunshine will speed up this process).
3. When the message is dry, your friend can decode it. (It's a good idea to decode the message over a sink.) While one person holds the paper, the other person should light the match and sweep it in small circles about an inch under the paper. Be careful not to hold the match in one place for more than a second. After a few moments, the secret message will appear.

Why?

The lemon juice contains a chemical that burns much more quickly than paper. So, before the paper has a chance to heat and ignite, the lemon juice burns, revealing the secret message.

PARENTAL SUPERVISION RECOMMENDED
Your brain is constantly trying to make sense of the information it receives. In the next experiment, you will be able to *see* your brain trying to sort out confusing visual images.

What You'll Need

- 8½" x 11" white construction paper
- ruler
- colored pens
- various household items with a circular edge, varying in size
- scissors
- 8½" x 11" sheet of paper
- a partner

Directions

1. First, create a "vision separator" for yourself. Hold the construction paper against your face and have a friend outline your profile (A).
2. Cut along the line, and you'll have a piece of paper that fits over your forehead, nose, and mouth that separates your vision.
3. Now draw a vertical line down the center of the sheet of paper.
4. Using two different-colored pens, draw two circles (the size of cola cans) on opposite sides of the line (B).
5. Place your vision separator along the vertical line of the paper, fit your profile into the separator, and look at the circles. What happens to them?
6. This is one you can play around with. Experiment by drawing the different shapes shown in C, or make up your own.

Why?

To determine an object's position correctly, your brain requires both of your eyes (stereoscopic vision). The vision separator took away your brain's ability to determine position. Because the images *looked* the same, and their position was unclear to your brain, your brain thought they were a single image. That's why it tried to fuse them.

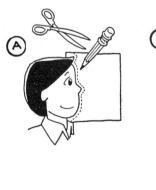

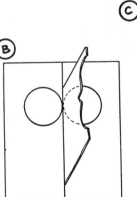

Your mind favors the familiar. That is, your brain sees what it is used to seeing. It loves patterns. For example, as you learned to read, your mind became familiar with common sentence structures and sounds. But your mind can trick you, and in the following experiments, we'll show you how. After you've played these word games, try them on a friend or family member.

Directions

1. Read the following sign out loud.

> A frivolous feline of Fenwith,
> Donned her finest of furs to fetch men with.
> First the frog of St. Fly
> On the Fourth of July,
> Then the fish of Fifeshire on the Fifth.

2. Now count the number of f's in the limerick (before you read further). How many were there? Did you count sixteen? Seventeen? Would you believe there are actually twenty f's in the rhyme? Which ones did you miss?
3. Next read the following sign out loud.

4. Write what you read on a piece of paper. Now compare what you wrote against the sign. Are they the same? Look very carefully and you'll see that there are two "the's" in the phrase. Chances are you missed the second one both when you read it aloud and compared your written version against it.

Why?

If you're like most people, when you counted the f's in the first sign you missed the f's in each word "of." Because the word is pronounced as though it were spelled "ov," your mind literally did not see the "f" even though it was right in front of your nose.

In the second sign, you didn't see the second "the" because you're not used to seeing two "the's" in a row in English. In fact, your brain recognizes a different pattern: only one "the." So your mind skips right over the second "the"!

Know Your Way

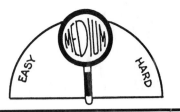

PARENTAL SUPERVISION RECOMMENDED
Next time you go backpacking or hiking, bring a needle, a magnet, and matches. If you ever become lost and no one has a compass, you'll be a hero!

What You'll Need

- cork (about ½″ wide)
- horseshoe magnet (6-lb pull)
- knife
- match
- needle
- pencil

Directions

1. Cut off the bottom end of your cork (like you're slicing a carrot). Then cut a notch down the center of the flat side of your cork chip.
2. Press the needle lengthwise into the notch.
3. Light a match and heat one end of the needle until it is hot. Then touch it to your magnet (A).
4. Dip the needle into the water to cool it, then drop your cork chip into the center of the bowl of water, with the needle side down. What happens? You've made a compass!
5. Using a pencil point, rotate the needle away from its position, then let go. Your compass will spin back to north. Hold a magnet around and above the compass and watch what happens (B).

Why?

Heating the needle makes it easier for the little north and south poles inside the needle to line up with the magnet's poles. When it cools, the poles stay lined up, leaving the needle magnetized.

Ⓐ HEAT NEEDLE, THEN TOUCH TO MAGNET

Ⓑ

Static Charge

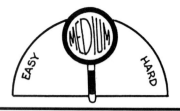

Almost everything you experience results from a quality of microscopic particles called "charge." Charged particles are responsible for the strange attractions and repulsions between objects. Moving charges create magnetic forces, while static charges create electric forces.

What You'll Need

- a plastic rod (acrylic or plexiglass, 1 ft. long x ½" wide)
- a silk scarf
- sheet of notebook paper
- rubber glove

Directions

1. Tear up the sheet of paper into tiny bits. Spread the bits on a table so they're not touching each other.
2. Put a rubber glove on one hand and hold the plastic rod with it. With the other hand, rub the silk scarf vigorously up and down along the rod for a few seconds.
3. Hold the rod close to the paper bits. What happens? Move the rod in circles over the paper bits and watch them dance and fly!
4. Experiment by moving the paper bits nearer and farther apart on the table. Don't forget to rub the rod now and then with the silk.

Why?

When it comes to charged particles, it's true that opposites attract. A negative charge attracts a positive charge, and vice versa. When it comes to *same* charges, though, the attraction is over. Two negative charges repel (push away) each other, as do two positive charges.

The plastic rod and silk were chosen for this experiment because of their natural qualities. When you rub the plastic with the silk, the plastic strips off negatively charged particles (electrons) from the silk. Thus, by rubbing the rod you are "charging" it. The rubber glove prevents the charged particles from coming off the rod onto your hand.

When you approach the paper bits, the negative charges on the rod attract the positive charges in the paper. The paper leaps up to the rod (so fast, though, that you have to watch carefully to see it). Once the paper and rod touch, however, the negative charges on the rod rapidly leak onto the paper. (Can you guess why? Because the negative charges on the rod are trying to get away from each other!) Some of the paper immediately becomes negatively charged. Given that same charges push each other away, what would you expect to happen next? The paper and rod repel each other. The rod is too heavy to go anywhere, but the paper bits are light enough to shoot away.

Wonder List

- Try holding up the charged rod to your hair. It's also fun to go into a dark room and hold the tip of the charged rod to your finger.

Creating a Force Field

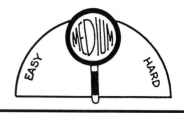

What do magnets and electricity have in common? Plenty! They're different aspects of the same physical structure. Create a magnetic field and see.

What You'll Need

- two D-size batteries
- the compass you made in Know Your Way
- insulated wire, 20″ long (22-gauge "bus" wire or larger, stripped ½″ on either end)
- tape
- bowl of water

Directions

1. Tape the two batteries together, positive end to negative end.
2. Coil the center of the wire around your finger and twist it once. Leave about three inches of wire free at either end, and tape these ends to the metal ends of the batteries.
3. Fill a bowl with water and drop in the needle compass you made.
4. Dip the loop of wire into the water and watch what happens to your compass. This time you've made a magnetic force field!

Why?

In your experiment, the battery pushed charged particles (electrons) through the coil of wire. These moving electrical charges created a magnetic field, which could affect the compass you made. In a simple magnet, this is exactly what happens. The charged particles move within the iron and create a force field that attracts metal objects.

38 The Human Antenna

What You'll Need

- television set
- screwdriver
- a human body (you'll do nicely)

Directions

1. Turn your television on and tune in to a station with clear reception.
2. Your television set has two antenna connections labeled "VHF" (which stands for very high frequency) on the back. Using the screwdriver, loosen these connections and detach the antenna wires. What happens to the picture on the screen? Your TV reception should be distorted and snowy.
3. Have a friend or parent watch the screen as you perform the next step. Extend your left arm out to the side, and, using the index finger of your right hand, touch one of the two connections.
4. Now switch places with your partner and repeat Step 3. What happens to the picture when your partner touches the screw?

Why?

An antenna is a device that collects electromagnetic signals and then sends them to an "electronic box" to be decoded—in this case, your television set. The larger the antenna, the more signals it can collect. The screw on the back of your television set is too small to collect many of the signals, so the reception is poor. Your body, however, can collect many more signals. By touching the screw, your body can then send them to the television's electronics, resulting in a much better picture.

Wonder List

- In astronomy, why are bigger telescopes better?
- Did you know that your eye behaves like a miniature antenna? It collects electromagnetic information (in the form of light), and the pupil, by getting larger or smaller, controls the amount of information coming in.

Stop the Music

All around you at every moment there is information in the air waiting to be decoded. Music and pictures from faraway lands, tales of distant galaxies, the life and death of stars—all this and more exist in the form of electromagnetic waves, the kind of waves picked up by a radio, television, or telescope. Most of the time, this wave energy goes unnoticed. But with the right kind of "magic box," you can explore new worlds. In the next two experiments, we will explore some of the properties of these waves, and we'll answer two questions concerning this invisible realm: Is it ever possible to escape these mysterious waves? Can the waves really travel through you?

What You'll Need

- a transistor radio (battery operated)
- aluminum foil

Directions

1. Turn your radio on and tune it to a station that has a clear signal.
2. Now tear a piece of aluminum foil long enough to completely wrap the radio, including the antenna.
3. Sit the radio on top of the foil, then slowly raise the sides of the foil until they meet and overlap above the radio. What happened to the reception? Why did the radio stop playing?

Why?

A radio is a "magic box" that selects particular waves out of the shower of electromagnetic waves around us. One way to shield out radio waves is to surround the radio with a conductor (a metal, such as the aluminum foil). The charged particles in the conductor move around in response to the waves to neutralize them. When the waves are neutralized, your radio suddenly has no more information to decode.

By the way, have you ever noticed that plug-in radios don't have antennas? That's because the cord acts as an antenna. Signals from space can reach your radio through the electrical wiring in your home into the radio cord. To "stop the music," you'd have to shield your entire home!

Wonder List

- If people from another planet were trying to communicate with us, what kind of "magic box" would we have to build to hear them?*

- Signals reaching us from distant galaxies and stars allow us to see back in time—wow!

*This question is too fascinating to leave unanswered. As a matter of fact, scientists have developed a superhuge radio telescope for just the purpose of "hearing" signals from other planets. The program is called the Search for Extra-Terrestrial Intelligence, or SETI for short.

The Invisible Made Visible

You will see mysterious magnetic forces at work in this experiment.

What You'll Need

- horseshoe magnet (6-lb pull)
- sheet of heavy construction paper or thin cardboard
- iron filings
- a partner

Directions

1. It's best to work over a table on this one. Start by holding the construction paper horizontally with one hand.
2. With your other hand, hold the magnet underneath the paper with the end of the horseshoe facing up.
3. Have a partner slowly pour the iron filings onto the paper in a sweeping fashion. Notice the very particular pattern the filings fall into.
4. Slide the magnet all around the underside of the paper. Carefully observe how the magnet affects the filings. How would you describe their behavior as you move the magnet?

Why?

Iron is a magnetic material, which means that it can be affected (pushed or pulled) by another magnet. A big piece of iron would be too heavy to be pushed or pulled by a small magnet, but the tiny iron filings in your experiment were light enough to move easily in response to the magnetic forces of the magnet. When you poured the filings onto a piece of paper held close to the magnet, you made a map of a portion of its "magnetic field"—that is, the region of space affected by the magnet. This magnetic field is usually invisible, but by pouring the filings you made the invisible visible!

Wonder List

- Would sawdust react to a magnet the way iron filings do? Why are some materials magnetic and others not? What mysterious things go on inside a magnet?
- In a compass, where is the magnet making the compass needle point north? Can you guess what it is? It's the earth! The earth happens to be a gigantic magnet.

Hot Socks

Have you ever wondered why people wear light-colored clothes in the summertime? Did you ever stand barefoot on a hot asphalt playground and then run like mad to find relief on the white lines? In the following experiment, you will observe and understand why black heats up in the presence of light.

What You'll Need

- a pair of white socks
- a pair of black socks
- a bright lamp, with removable shade (optional)

Directions

1. You'll need a warm sunny day for this one (but a strong lamp will do if a sunny day refuses to appear). Start by putting your black socks on one hand and foot, and the white socks on the other hand and foot.
2. Find a spot where the sunshine is clear and strong, sit in a comfortable position with your feet stretched out, and read about some of the other experiments in this book. Notice anything happening to the hand and foot with the black socks on? (You can achieve the same effect by holding your sock-covered hands about four or five inches away from a 100-watt light bulb. Be sure not to stare at the light!)

Why?

In the Reflections on Colors experiment, we showed that "black" really means that a substance is absorbing all colors of light and reflecting none. The light being absorbed has energy (it comes from the sun). When it is collected, this energy can heat things up. Thus, the black sock (the asphalt, black clothing, etc.) absorbs and collects the light energy and heats up your foot. On the other hand, the white sock (the white painted lines, white clothing, etc.) reflects most of the light (and its energy) away from you.

Wonder List

- We usually think of outer space as extremely cold, so why do the astronauts wear white space suits?

The Light Barrier

We know that electric current flows through metal, but will it flow through water? You can rig up a flashlight to answer that question.

What You'll Need

- flashlight
- two 10″ pieces of insulated wire (22-gauge)
- clear glass bowl
- distilled water
- salt
- measuring spoons
- a partner
- tape
- two copper plates

Directions

1. Unscrew and remove the flashlight lid and take the contents out. Tape the two batteries together (positive end to negative end).
2. Have an adult strip ½″ of the insulation off both ends of both wires.
3. Tape one wire end to the negative end of your two batteries. Tape another wire end (from the second piece of wire) to the circle of metal (usually copper) in the light bulb piece.
4. With a long piece of tape, attach the flashlight bulb to the positive battery end as shown. Test that your flashlight works by touching the two free wire ends together. (It's okay to touch these exposed ends; not enough current is traveling through them to do any harm.)
5. Have a friend hold the copper plates in the bowl. Now touch the free wire ends to the plates. Does your flashlight flash on?
6. Add salt slowly and watch what happens.

Why?

A material allows electric current to flow (or conduct) when there are charged particles (electrons) inside it that are free to move. In a normal light bulb, for example, the electrons in the bulb's tiny wire (called the filament) can flow easily. This flow heats the filament until it glows white hot and the bulb shines. However, when the electrons inside a material are held tightly in place, no current can flow. This is what happens with distilled water, which is an insulator (it cannot conduct electrons). Adding salt stripped some electrons away from the water, allowing them to move around the copper plates, then through the wires to the filament to light the bulb.

TOUCH WIRES TO PLATES

HOLD COPPER PLATES IN WATER

Don't Take Sides

PARENTAL SUPERVISION RECOMMENDED

We usually think of objects as having at least two sides. For example, a piece of paper has a front and a back, and a loop has an inside and an outside. Do you think it is possible for something to have only one side? We're going to make the famous Möbius strip (named for its inventor) and see.

What You'll Need

- sheet of construction paper
- scissors
- pen, pencil, or colored marker
- ruler
- transparent tape

Directions

1. Cut a strip of paper that is 1″ wide and 10½″ long.
2. With the ruler and pen or pencil, mark off sections on the strip of paper. Your first mark should be ¼″ from the left end of the strip. Draw a vertical line through it. From there, tick off 1″ increments until you reach the other end of the strip, where you'll have ¼″ remaining. There, draw another vertical line (A).
3. Now number your inches 1 through 10 as shown. Take the bottom of the strip and flip it up and over to the other side of the strip.
4. Repeat steps 2 and 3, this time numbering the inches from 11 to 20.
5. Now, holding the ends of the strip, twist it once, then join the ends. Overlap the ends exactly ¼″ and tape the ends in place on both "sides" (B).
6. Voilà! You've just created a loop with only one side. How did you do it? If you don't believe you've got a one-sided loop, count the numbers on your strip starting with 1. When you reach 11, the opposite side of your strip, you'll find no flipping is required to keep counting to 20.

Wonder List

- Can you think of anything else with just one side?*

*Neither can we.

Ⓐ

10½″

1″ | 1 2 3 4 5 6 7 8 9 10

¼″ **MARK OFF IN ONE-INCH INCREMENTS** ¼″

Ⓑ

**TWIST
AND TAPE
ENDS TOGETHER**

Musical Bottles

Have you ever wondered why the tuba, with its booming voice, is such a large instrument, and why the piccolo, with its tiny voice, is such a small instrument? What does sound have to do with size? Let's see. . . .

What You'll Need

- six empty glass bottles (same size)
- water

Directions

1. Fill the bottles with varying amounts of water, from nearly empty to nearly full. Then line the bottles up as shown (A).
2. Blow across the top of each bottle, one by one, starting with the bottle with the least water. What happens to the sound pitch as you move from bottle to bottle?
3. Now repeat your music-making, this time moving fast as you blow across your row of bottles in one breath.

Why?

Sound is actually vibrations, or waves, in the air. The faster the waves vibrate, the higher the sound pitch. The slower they vibrate, the deeper the sound pitch. How long or short the waves are has to do with how fast or slow they vibrate. The rapidly vibrating, high-pitched waves are short, while the slowly vibrating, low-pitched waves are long. If the waves have a large space to vibrate in, they will be longer than if they have a small space to vibrate in.

A good way to see this is by taking hold of one end of a garden hose (leaving the other end attached to the faucet) and shaking it up and down. When you shake the full length of the hose, the vibrations in it are slow and long. (If the vibrations were sound, the hose would have a deep voice!) When you shake a shorter length of hose (say, shorter by ten feet), you'll see that the vibrations are faster and shorter. (Here the hose would have a higher voice.)

This is exactly what happened in your musical bottles. The larger the space in which the air could vibrate, the longer and slower were the vibrations (B). So, the deepest sound came from the bottle with the least amount of water and the most air. The smaller the space in which the air could vibrate, the shorter and higher were the vibrations (B). So, the highest sound came from the bottle with the most water and the least air.

Wonder List

- Compare the sounds made by a bottle being filled with those of a bottle being emptied. The "glug-glug" sounds of the first will start low and end high. And of the second?

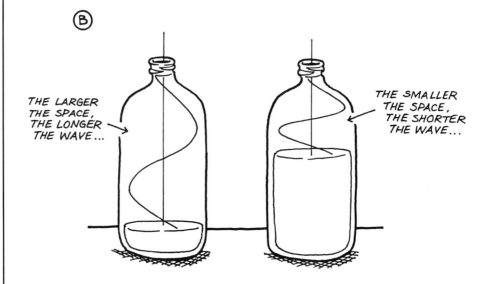

Ⓑ

THE LARGER
THE SPACE,
THE LONGER
THE WAVE...

THE SMALLER
THE SPACE,
THE SHORTER
THE WAVE...

Learning Topsoil Conservation

PARENTAL SUPERVISION RECOMMENDED

Before they knew that topsoil was the most valuable soil for agriculture, farmers used to let topsoil wash away. Much fertile land was destroyed. You can see for yourself how this might have happened by comparing an old farming method with a new one designed to conserve topsoil.

What You'll Need

- two half-gallon milk cartons
- two books (or pieces of wood) each about an inch thick
- scissors
- two sprinkling cans (or pitchers)
- two buckets
- dirt or potting soil
- ruler
- a partner
- water

Directions

1. Cut off one side and the top of the two milk cartons. Then cut the remaining sides and bottoms so they're four inches high.
2. Fill your cartons with dirt and shape it into mounds that taper down at the open end of the carton. Set the cartons at the edge of a table, the back ends on books, and place the two buckets below to catch dirt and mud.
3. In carton 1, furrow three parallel lines down the length of the dirt mound. In carton 2, furrow one winding, continuous line.
4. Now your miniature "farms" are ready for a rainstorm. With a partner assisting you, simultaneously trickle about a pint of water from the sprinkling cans into both cartons. Which "farm" holds the most water?

Why?

Carton 2 demonstrates the modern "contour" farming method. Since the furrow is longer, it is better on two counts: the water has more time to be absorbed by the dirt, and less topsoil is washed away. If you lift both cartons, carton 2 will feel heavier because the dirt was able to absorb more water.

Super Sleuth

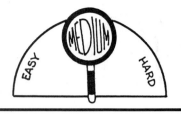

EASY MEDIUM HARD

Here's an experiment that will let you play detective and teach you something about a very important tool in crime investigation—fingerprinting.

What You'll Need

- one teaspoon fine carbon powder (if necessary, a piece of charcoal ground up with a mortar and pestle or hammer will do)
- mixing bowl and spoon
- a fine-haired cosmetic brush
- transparent tape
- white paper
- ceramic plate or blow
- one teaspoon baking soda
- magnifying glass

Directions

1. In a mixing bowl, combine the baking soda and carbon and mix thoroughly.
2. Now you or your partner gets to play international jewel thief and leave your fingerprints behind. A ceramic plate or bowl works well for this. (By the way, newly washed hands will not leave the best of prints behind.)
3. With your magnifying glass, inspect for fingerprints. Find anything?
4. Now dip the cosmetic brush into the carbon mixture and *very lightly* dust the ceramic surface. Inspect the area with your magnifying glass. Now what do you see?
5. Place a piece of tape over the fingerprint to "lift" it. Rub the tape gently, then place the tape on a piece of white paper. You should have a close-to-perfect fingerprint for your crime files. Make fingerprints of several people and line them up to compare.

Why?

The natural oils in your hands stick to surfaces, leaving fingerprints behind. The oils aren't very visible, but the carbon mixture clinging to the oils is. Since no two fingerprints are alike, when a set of prints is found during a criminal investigation, there can be no doubt who the culprit is!

Show Me the Light

PARENTAL SUPERVISION RECOMMENDED

What will a plant do when deprived of most of its sunlight? Like all living things, it has to adapt to its new environment. In the following experiment, you will see for yourself what we mean.

What You'll Need

- a syngonium "arrow leaf" plant from your local nursery
- scissors or knife
- cardboard box, tall enough to cover the plant without bending the leaves
- sheet of notebook paper
- pen or pencil

Directions

1. First cut a 3″ square "window" in one side of the box.
2. Now find a sunny spot indoors where you can leave your plant undisturbed for several days. Carefully observe the position of your plant's leaves. In which direction are they facing? They should be facing all different directions. Note the information on the paper, which you can call your "Helio Log" (*helio* in Greek means "sun").
3. Now place the box over the plant. Note on the log the date and time you covered the plant as well as the direction the window is facing. Keep your plant covered at all times, except for the few moments when the syngonium may need watering. No peeking!
4. Here you get a break from this experiment. Go try the next experiment—it's fun!
5. After approximately 48 hours, uncover your plant. Notice anything different about the leaves? How and why have the leaves shifted direction? Record your observations in your Helio Log.

Why?

You can think of sunlight as the food of plants. Without sunlight, plants will neither grow nor live long. Through a process called photosynthesis, plants convert sunlight energy into a form they can use as food. In this sense, sunlight is not unlike the oxygen that we need to survive (see the Fuel for

Thought experiment). When imprisoned in the darkness of a box, your plant was literally starved of nutrition. So, naturally, it had to adapt to its new environment. To drink up the only sunlight available, the plant turned its broad leaves toward the window. How long do you think your plant could survive with only this windowful of light?

Wonder List

- Why is it that the foliage of most trees is not at the base or even the middle of the tree, but at their very tip-tops?

Fuel for Thought

PARENTAL SUPERVISION RECOMMENDED
When you see a lighted candle, the wick is the fuel for the flame. Is that all the candle needs to burn?

What You'll Need

- candle
- matches
- a clear glass, tall enough to fit over candle

Directions

1. Light the candle.
2. Place the glass over the candle. Can you guess what will happen to the flame?

Why?

A burning candle is a chemical reaction. Like many other reactions, it needs oxygen to continue. In this experiment, the flame went out because it needed oxygen to continue burning the fuel (the wick).

Wonder List

- A burning candle is much like human metabolism. Metabolism is the process by which food and other substances are converted into energy that the body can use. Oxygen is a very important part of that process, and without it, metabolism couldn't occur.

Mystical Crystals

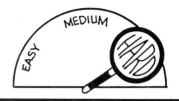

PARENTAL SUPERVISION REQUIRED

Have you ever seen a glistening geode with its lavender, green, or blue crystals sparkling in the light? Crystals are among the most beautiful of all structures. Their very precise shape comes from the precise way in which their atoms stack up like building blocks. Other substances such as glass have no such regularity, so they lack the special crystalline appearance.

What You'll Need

- 500-ml Erlenmeyer flask (with rubber stopper)
- sodium acetate, powdered, with no impurities (nontoxic)
- ice cubes
- funnel
- measuring spoons
- flashlight
- stove burner
- water
- 8″ test tube (with 8-cup volume)
- plastic straw
- tall glass
- glove potholder

Directions

1. Fill the flask half full with water and set it on a stove burner at medium heat. You'll want the water to be boiling by the time you get to step 4.
2. Make a "solution" (a mixture) of water and sodium acetate (which is a kind of salt). Pour two tablespoons of lukewarm water into the test tube.
3. Now, using the funnel and measuring spoon, bit by bit pour three-and-a-half teaspoons of the sodium acetate into the test tube. After pouring each teaspoon, cover the tube with the stopper and shake. You'll find that by the time you get to the last half teaspoon, your solution is "saturated," and not all of the salt will dissolve.
4. Next, drop the test tube into the Erlenmeyer flask with boiling water in it (A). After a couple of minutes, pour another four-and-a-half teaspoons of the sodium acetate into the solution. Stir the mixture with the straw after each teaspoon to dissolve the salt.
5. Place two ice cubes in a tall glass of water. Then, with the potholder, lift the test tube out of the flask and place it in the glass (B).
6. After 90 seconds, drop a small pinch of the salt into the test tube and watch what happens (C). Don't take your eyes off the tube. Hold the flashlight up to the crystals. Wow!

Ⓐ

61

7. To repeat the experiment, just return the test tube to the flask, watch the crystals melt, then repeat steps 5 and 6.

Just as a building needs a first block to build on, a crystal needs its first block to build on. The building blocks for crystals are usually tiny particles. When you first poured the sodium acetate into the water, the water molecules grabbed on to the salt atoms, and the salt disappeared. But at a low temperature, the water can grab on to only so much salt. To get it to grab on to even more salt, you needed to increase the water temperature. So, as the water became hotter, it could pull even more salt atoms into the solution.
You then cooled the solution in the glass of cold water. All the salt that wouldn't dissolve at the lower temperature suddenly became available to make crystals. Here is where the building blocks came in: Before the salt atoms could make crystals, they needed something to grab on to (build on). Pinching in a bit of the salt provided the first block on which the salt crystal could grow. Once that happened, another crystal could build onto the first, and then another onto the second, and then in a matter of seconds, presto! Crystals . . .

• All of computer electronics is based on the controlled growth of crystals. Have you heard of silicon? It's a crystal!

Ⓑ

Ⓒ

ADD PINCH OF
SODIUM ACETATE
AND WATCH!

SODIUM
ACETATE

Cloud in a Jar

PARENTAL SUPERVISION RECOMMENDED

Clouds are amazing things. One minute the sky is clear, and the next minute an immense cloud is looming toward you. They can be wispy or billowy, dangerous or harmless. But how do clouds form? Let's make one and see.

What You'll Need

- piece of rubber ⅓″ to ¼″ thick, cut in a circle to fit within the rubber ring inside pickle jar lid
- matches
- needle valve (for blowing up basketballs, etc.) and pump
- stick incense
- a glass pickle jar
- a partner
- hammer and nail

Directions

1. Nail two holes in the jar lid, one toward the outside of the lid (the "finger hole"), one in the center (the "valve hole") (A). Punch these holes from the inside out.
2. Push the nail through the center of the rubber to make a narrow hole.
3. Now put the needle valve first through the valve hole in the lid, then all the way through the rubber hole (B).
4. Attach the pump to the needle valve.
5. Put about one-half inch of water in the jar and swish it around.
6. With the jar held tilted at an angle, light the incense and stick it inside the jar for about three seconds (C). Then quickly pull it out and place the lid on the smoke-filled jar.

Ⓐ

VALVE HOLE

FINGER HOLE

Ⓑ

RUBBER CIRCLE

NEEDLE VALVE

7. Have your partner hold the jar and cover the finger hole tightly. Then, pump air into it five times. The smoke will clear as you pump.
8. As you watch the jar very carefully, have your partner uncover the finger hole. Poof!

Why?

Clouds form when the air pressure and temperature in the atmosphere drop suddenly. This allows condensation, or the formation of water droplets from vapor, to occur. (You can see condensation form on a glass of cold water left standing in a warm room.) But just like crystals in the previous experiment, the water vapor in the air needs something to grab on to (usually dust or soot) before it can become a water droplet. The smoke particles in your experiment supplied the building blocks for the droplets. The water vapor in the jar wanted to condense into droplets, but it couldn't because the air pressure was too high. Releasing some of the air out of the jar (by uncovering the finger hole) caused a sudden drop in pressure and temperature and . . . pop! A cloud was born.

- In drought-stricken areas, farmers will sometimes purposely "seed" a cloud by dropping solid particles into it. The water vapor in the cloud will condense onto the particles and form water droplets—rain!

- Would you guess that among the most disastrous aftereffects of a volcanic eruption are mudflows? Why?

ⒸLET SMOKE FILL ABOUT 3 SECONDS

STICK INCENSE

ABOUT ½ INCH OF WATER